Asteroids

by Derek Zobel

Consultant:
Duane Quam, M.S. Physics
Chair, Minnesota State
Academic Science Standards
Writing Committee

BLASTOFF!
READERS
3

BELLWETHER MEDIA • MINNEAPOLIS, MN

Note to Librarians, Teachers, and Parents:

Blastoff! Readers are carefully developed by literacy experts and combine standards-based content with developmentally appropriate text.

Level 1 provides the most support through repetition of high-frequency words, light text, predictable sentence patterns, and strong visual support.

Level 2 offers early readers a bit more challenge through varied simple sentences, increased text load, and less repetition of high-frequency words.

Level 3 advances early-fluent readers toward fluency through increased text and concept load, less reliance on visuals, longer sentences, and more literary language.

Level 4 builds reading stamina by providing more text per page, increased use of punctuation, greater variation in sentence patterns, and increasingly challenging vocabulary.

Level 5 encourages children to move from "learning to read" to "reading to learn" by providing even more text, varied writing styles, and less familiar topics.

Whichever book is right for your reader, Blastoff! Readers are the perfect books to build confidence and encourage a love of reading that will last a lifetime!

This edition first published in 2010 by Bellwether Media, Inc..

No part of this publication may be reproduced in whole or in part without written permission of the publisher. For information regarding permission, write to Bellwether Media, Inc., Attention: Permissions Department, 5357 Penn Avenue South, Minneapolis, MN 55419.

Library of Congress Cataloging-in-Publication Data

Zobel, Derek, 1983-
Asteroids / by Derek Zobel.
    p. cm. – (Blastoff! readers. exploring space)
Includes bibliographical references and index.
 Summary: "Introductory text and full-color images explore the physical characteristics of asteroids in space. Intended for students in kindergarten through third grade"–Provided by publisher.
ISBN 978-1-60014-196-6 (hardcover : alk. paper)
 1. Asteroids–Juvenile literature. I. Title.
QB651.Z63 2010
523.44–dc22   2009037943

Text copyright © 2010 by Bellwether Media, Inc.
Printed in the United States of America, North Mankato, MN.

010110   1149

Contents

Asteroids are rocks in the **solar system**. They **orbit** the sun. There are millions of asteroids in the solar system.

Most of them are shaped like potatoes. All of them have **craters**. Craters are caused by crashes with other objects.

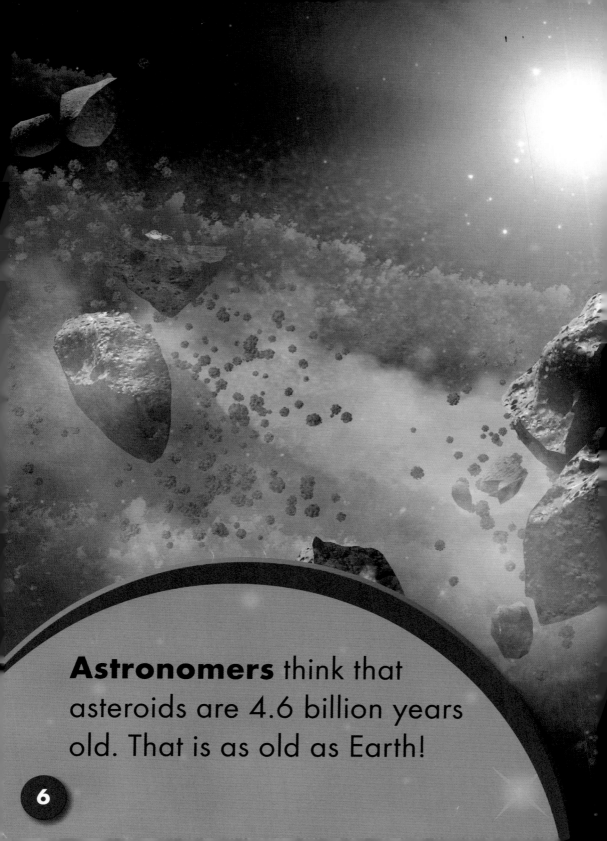

Astronomers think that asteroids are 4.6 billion years old. That is as old as Earth!

Asteroids hit each other over time and broke into smaller pieces. They continue to hit each other and break apart today.

Ceres

Asteroids range in size. The largest asteroid is Ceres. It is 584 miles (940 kilometers) across.

The smallest asteroids have diameters that are less than 1 mile (1.6 kilometers).

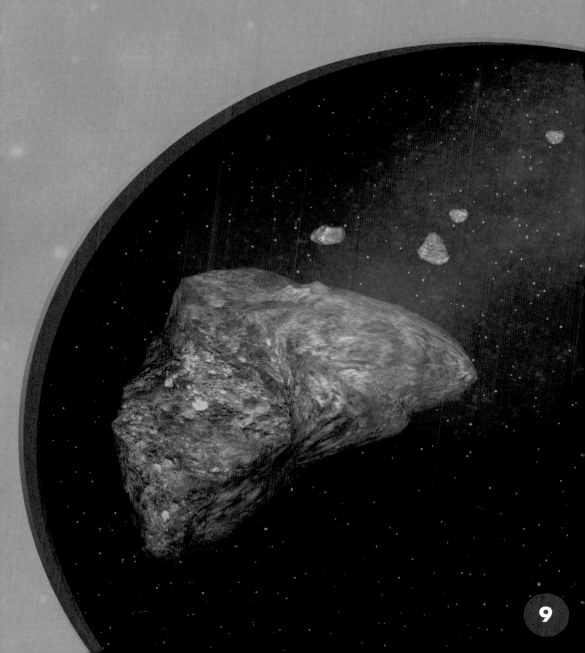

Most asteroids in the solar system are part of the **asteroid belt**. This belt lies between the orbits of Jupiter and Mars.

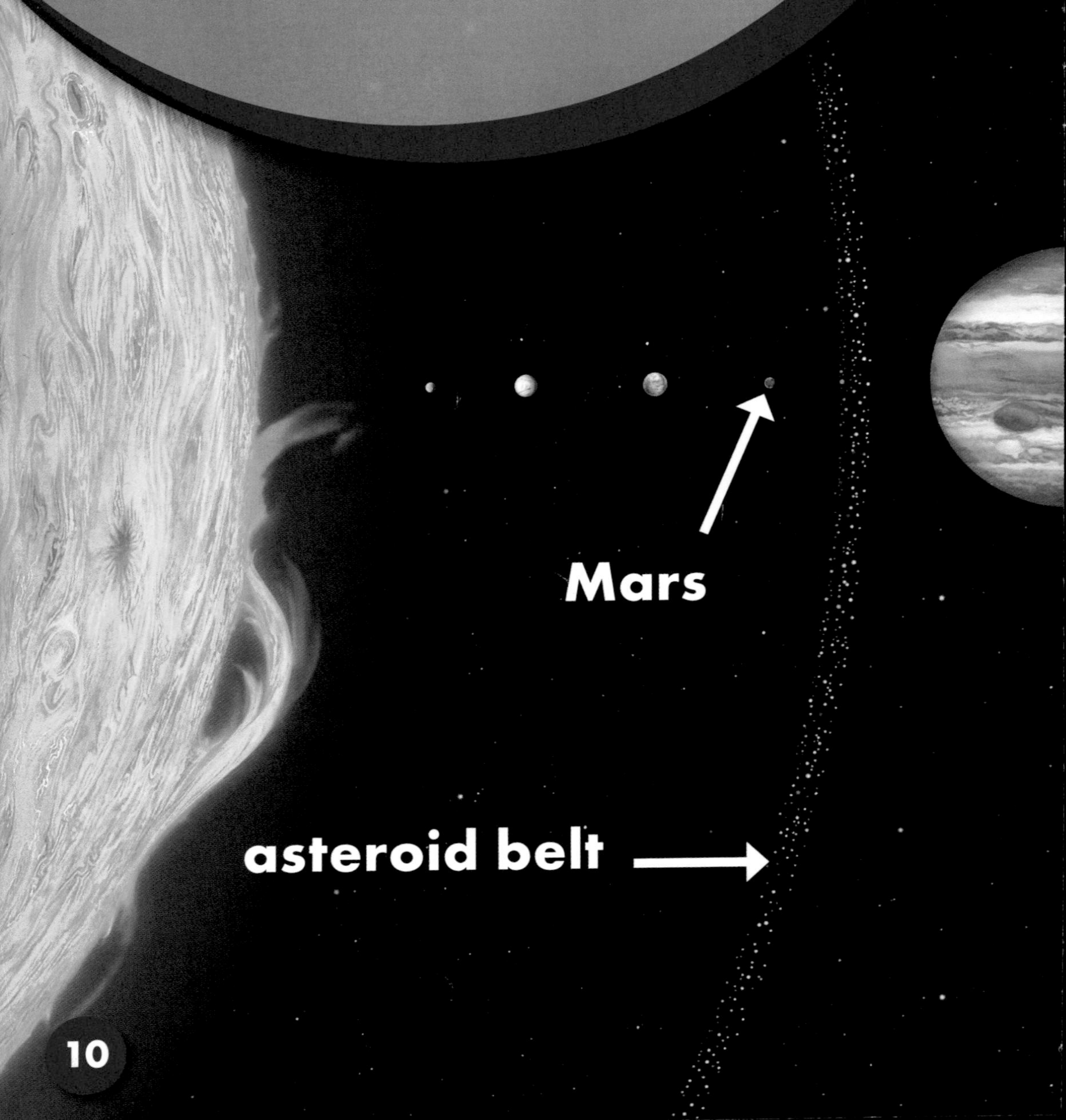

Mars

asteroid belt →

Jupiter

Jupiter and Mars can affect asteroids in the asteroid belt. They can pull asteroids out of their normal orbits.

Asteroids are made up of many kinds of materials.

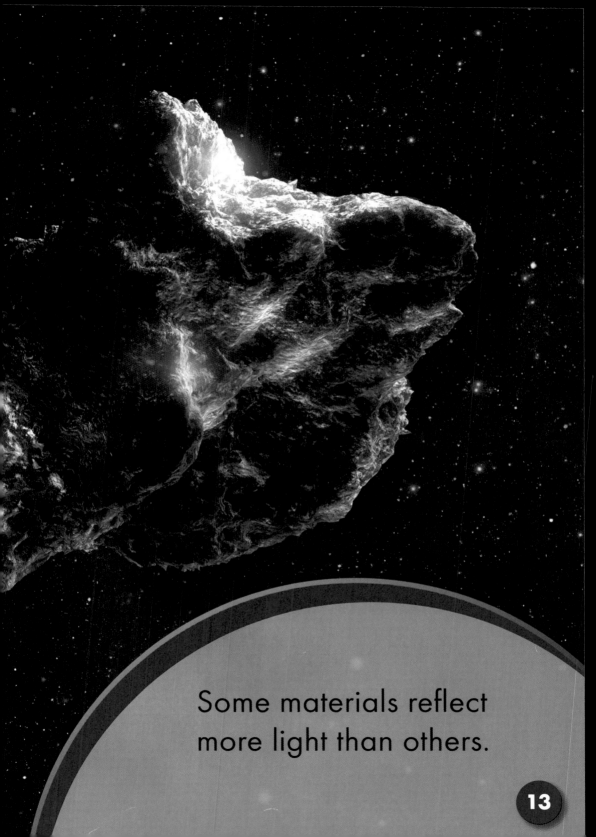

Some materials reflect
more light than others.

Some asteroids are made of
metals such as iron and nickel.
These asteroids look bright.

Others are made of **carbon**.
These asteroids look dark.

Giuseppe Piazzi discovered the first asteroid in 1801. He named it Ceres. He thought he had discovered a new planet.

Ceres

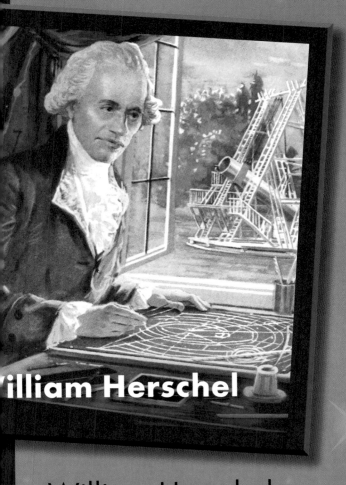

William Herschel

William Herschel was the first scientist to use the term *asteroid*. He used it in 1802. *Asteroid* is Greek for "star-like."

Scientists have discovered many asteroids since then. Some have been discovered with **telescopes**.

Galileo

Space probes have found other asteroids. *Galileo* was a space probe that found some asteroids with their own moons!

Scientists landed a space probe on an asteroid in 2001. The spacecraft sent back information about the orbit, size, and the materials that made up the asteroid.

Scientists hope that one day **astronauts** will land on an asteroid. They will learn even more about these large space rocks.

Glossary

asteroid belt—a ring of asteroids around the sun between the orbits of Jupiter and Mars

astronauts—people who have been trained to fly aboard a spacecraft and work in space

astronomers—scientists who study space and objects in space

carbon—a material found in all plants and animals

craters—holes made when meteorites or other space objects crash into moons, planets, asteroids, or other space objects

Galileo—a space probe sent to study asteroids and the planet Jupiter; it is named after the Italian astronomer Galileo Galilei.

orbit—to travel around the sun or other object in space

solar system—the sun and all the objects that orbit it; the solar system has planets, moons, comets, and asteroids.

space probes—spacecraft that explore planets and other space objects and send information back to Earth; space probes do not carry people.

telescopes—tools that make faraway objects look larger and nearer; large telescopes can see deep into space.

To Learn More

AT THE LIBRARY

Bonar, Samantha. *Asteroids.* New York, N.Y.: Franklin Watts, 2000.

Sherman, Josepha. *Asteroids, Comets, and Meteors.* New York, N.Y.: Benchmark Books, 2009.

Sparrow, Giles. *Asteroids, Comets, and Meteors.* Chicago, Ill.: Heinemann Library, 2002.

ON THE WEB

Learning more about asteroids is as easy as 1, 2, 3.

1. Go to www.factsurfer.com.

2. Enter "asteroids" into the search box.

3. Click the "Surf" button and you will see a list of related Web sites.

With factsurfer.com, finding more information is just a click away.

BLASTOFF! JIMMY CHALLENGE

Blastoff! Jimmy is hidden somewhere in this book. Can you find him? If you need help, you can find a hint at the bottom of page 24.

Index

The images in this book are reproduced through the courtesy of: Juan Martinez, front cover, pp. 14, 21;
NASA, pp. 4 (small), 6-7, 20; Chris Butler / Photo Researchers, Inc., pp. 4-5, 8, 10-11, 16-17; Megall
| Dreamstime.com, p. 9; Sebastian Kaulitzki, pp. 12-13, 15, 18-19; The Print Collector, p. 17 (small);
Christophe Lehanaff, p. 18 (small).

Blastoff! Jimmy Challenge (from page 23).
Hint: Go to page 6 to catch a break.